PAul and JAMES

Were They Really In Agreement?

*A SCRIPTURAL EXPLANATION
OF THE DIFFERING VIEWS OF
PAUL AND JAMES*

BRAD ROBERTSON
Author of *The Story of Grace,
Addicted To Grace, and Strategic Church*

Paul and James: Were They Really In Agreement?

A scriptural explanation of the differing views of Paul and James on justification.

Paul and James: Were They Really In Agreement?
Copyright ©2020 by Brad Robertson

First Edition - 2020

ISBN   9798648690059 (KDP)

Printed In The United States of America

Introduction

Often, when teaching on the book of James, Bible teachers and preachers attempt to convince us Paul and James are in agreement when it comes to justification. The reason they do this is because it is very obvious they were not in agreement but in great disagreement. Because of this obvious disagreement between Paul and James, there is a conflict in Scripture in the minds of Bible teachers and preachers, leading them to the false conclusion that if Paul and James disagree, the Bible cannot be trusted. Consequently, they believe the entire Bible might as well then be thrown out, since, according to them, a Bible divided against itself cannot stand. As a result, Bible teachers and preachers seek to harmonize Paul's and James' teachings on justification.

The problem with this approach in interpreting the letter of James is that it is driven by fear of the Bible losing its credibility if Paul and James are not united in their understanding of justification. So rather than seeking the historical facts surrounding the views of Paul and James on justification, Bible teachers, in order to maintain their understanding of the Bible's credibility and unity, seek to justify their already preconceived conclusion that Paul and James are in total agreement. This preconceived conclusion results in a faulty approach when interpreting the book of James, producing faulty interpretations and applications.

Holding to an already preconceived belief before healthy principles of interpretation are applied is much like a scientist who has already concluded God doesn't exist; therefore, the scientist must seek to find another cause for the origins of life and universe. The proper way to discover the origins of life and the universe is to have no preconceived conclusions about the existence of God, but let the evidence gathered in the research process formulate one's beliefs about whether there is a God who created the universe. After studying the design of the human body, the design of biology, and the design of the universe, it is evident there is an intelligent design to it. This leads us to conclude there must be an intelligent mind behind it that some would call God.

NO PRECONCIEVED CONCLUSIONS

Just like scientists should not begin the process of seeking to discover the origins of the universe with a preconceived belief that God doesn't exist, we should not seek to interpret the letters of Paul and James having already concluded they are in complete agreement. Just as a biased approach taints the findings of a scientist searching for the origins of life and the universe, it will also taint the findings of one studying Scripture.

So to proceed through the learning process with honest study and to arrive at the end of the learning process with accurate conclusions, it is imperative one starts the learning process with no preconceived conclusions. Only then can findings be trusted.

STUDY THE BIBLE YOURSELF

For most of my life, I was taught about the Bible, of which I am so thankful. However, I have learned not everything

2

I was taught was accurate. Those who taught me were sincere in their teachings, but not everything they taught me was correct. For example, I was taught that to *fall from grace* meant a person fell out of good standing with God because they went back into a life of sin. Yet, in studying the Bible, I discovered to fall from grace was to go back into a religious and moral system seeking to gain a right standing with God (righteousness) through self-effort (see Galatians 5:4) rather than trusting in Christ alone.

The realization not everything Bible preachers and teachers communicate is biblically accurate motivated me to study the Bible for myself, paying attention to the historical, cultural, and biblical context of Scripture. I have come to the realization it is okay to not automatically accept the words of others as gospel truth, and it is okay to question them and study God's word for myself, even if it means my conclusions about some Bible verses may differ from theirs.

Through my personal study of the Bible, I have learned to take to the Bible what a preacher or teacher communicates to see if their words are in agreement with the Bible. There are times, after this evaluation, I have changed my personal understanding of certain Scriptures or doctrines to that of the teacher or preacher, since their view of that particular scripture or doctrine was biblical, whereas my previous understanding may have been based upon what was merely traditional.

Because of the freedom I have to study the Bible for myself, I no longer put these men or women on a pedestal. After all, they are only people who, like me, are filled with flaws and in need of grace. They are imperfect, just as I am. Therefore, they are not perfect in all their interpretations of Scripture.

Too often, we make the mistake of following a certain understanding of Scripture simply because it is taught by a Bible teacher or preacher we respect greatly. To question his or her understanding of Scripture can seem heretical and disrespectful. Also, if we question the views of another person's favorite Bible teacher or preacher, we are then highly criticized by the followers of this Bible teacher or preacher. For example, one time, in the presence of those who follow the teachings of John Piper, I questioned his interpretation of certain Bible verses. In doing so, I was highly criticized and strongly encouraged to *"get on board"* with what John Piper was teaching. They said, *"If John Piper teaches it, we must get on board with it. Who are we not to get on board with what John Piper teaches?"* Followers of John Piper were astonished I would not *"get on board"* with his interpretation of certain Bible verses.

This *"get on board"* mentality is dangerous. It's cultish. Please note, John Piper was not suggesting everyone *"get on board"* with his teaching simply because he teaches it. I am sure he is totally unaware of others telling me to *"get on board because John Piper teaches it."* Some of those promoting this dangerous, cultish act of *"getting on board"* were those who hold him in high regard as a Bible teacher. Yet, this doesn't mean he is beyond being questioned and disagreed with about something he may teach. I am sure he would welcome for his teachings to be honestly scrutinized and questioned by others. I am sure he would strongly oppose the *"get on board because John Piper teaches it"* mentality.

As you read through my own understanding of Paul's' and James' views on justification, please remember they are only the views of a flawed imperfect man in need of grace. My conclusions may be 100% wrong. The conclusions of other Bible teachers may be 100% right. My encouragement to you is that you study Scripture for yourself, never taking any Bible teacher's view, including my view, on any Scripture as the right view. Study God's word for yourself, without a preconceived bias, allowing the conclusion you eventually arrive at to be based on God's word not men's words.

With this in mind, here is my take on the views of Paul and James concerning justification.

ARE PAUL AND JAMES TEACHING THE SAME THING?

The major belief held by most Bible teachers and preachers is Paul and James are actually complementary of one another in that Paul talks about justification that comes by faith and James speaks of the works resulting from the faith that justifies. One popular way of explaining this is that Paul teaches on the root of justification, which is faith, and James focuses on the fruit of justification, which is works.

But are James and Paul really teaching the same about justification? Are they really in agreement? Are they really complimentary of one another? Or, is it possible they are in disagreement in what they taught on justification? And, if they are in disagreement, are there historical and biblical reasons for their disagreement? Furthermore, if they are not unified in their understanding of justification, does this mean the Bible has lost its credibility, making it no longer trustworthy? Then, since a Bible divided against itself cannot stand, as some Bible teachers believe, should we throw out the whole Bible?

It is my desire, in comparing the views of Paul and James, to answer these questions and to allow Scripture to speak for itself rather than allowing Bible teachers and preachers to speak for Scripture. By allowing Scripture to speak for itself, it can conclude for us if the teachings of Paul and James about justification are in agreement or disagreement, and if they are complementary or contradicting.

JUSTIFICATION DEFINED

Let's begin with defining justification.

Justification is the declaration of God where he pronounces a sinner, who is guilty of breaking his law, to be righteous or innocent the moment he places his faith in Jesus.

What is the basis for this declaration? What would move God to pronounce a sinner who is guilty of sin to be innocent in his sight when he places his faith in Jesus?

Let's compare from Scripture James' and Paul's teachings on justification.

PAUL'S TEACHING ON JUSTIFICATION

Acts 13:38-39

Therefore, my friends, I want you to know that through Jesus the forgiveness of sins is proclaimed to you. Through him everyone who believes is set free from every sin, a justification you were not able to obtain under the law of Moses.

Romans 3:21-24

But now apart from the law the righteousness of God has been made known, to which the Law and the Prophets testify. This righteousness is given through faith in Jesus Christ to all who believe. There is no difference between Jew and Gentile, for all have sinned and fall short of the glory of God, and all are justified freely by his grace through the redemption that came by Christ Jesus.

Romans 3:28

For we maintain that a person is justified by faith apart from the works of the law.

Romans 4:5-8

However, to the one who does not work but trusts God who justifies the ungodly, their faith is credited as righteousness. David says the same thing when he speaks of the blessedness of the one to whom God credits righteousness apart from works:

"Blessed are those

whose transgressions are forgiven,
whose sins are covered.
Blessed is the one
whose sin the Lord will never count against them."

Romans 4:24

...God will credit righteousness—for us who believe in him who raised Jesus our Lord from the dead. He was delivered over to death for our sins and was raised to life for our justification.

Romans 5:1-9

Therefore, since we have been justified through faith, we have peace with God through our Lord Jesus Christ, through whom we have gained access by faith into this grace in which we now stand. And we boast in the hope of the glory of God...You see, at just the right time, when we were still powerless, Christ died for the ungodly. Very rarely will anyone die for a righteous person, though for a good person someone might possibly dare to die. But God demonstrates his own love for us in this: While we were still sinners, Christ died for us. Since we have now been justified by his blood, how much more shall we be saved from God's wrath through him!

Romans 5:12-21

Therefore, just as sin entered the world through one man, and death through sin, and in this way death came to all people, because all sinned—To be sure, sin was in the world before the law was given, but sin is not charged against anyone's account where there is no law. Nevertheless, death reigned from the time of Adam to the time of Moses, even over those who did not sin by breaking a command, as did Adam, who is a pattern of the one to come. But the gift is not like the trespass. For if the many died by the trespass of the one man, how much more did God's grace and the gift that came by the grace of the one man, Jesus Christ, overflow to the many! Nor can the gift of God be compared with the result of one man's sin: The judgment followed one sin and brought condemnation, but the gift followed many trespasses and brought justification. For if, by the trespass of the one man, death reigned through that one man, how much more will those who receive God's abundant provision of grace and of the gift of righteousness reign in life through the one man, Jesus Christ! Consequently, just as one trespass resulted in condemnation for all people, so also one righteous act resulted in justification and life for all people. For just as through the disobedience of the one man the many were made sinners, so also through the obedience of the one man the many will be made righteous. The law was brought in so that the trespass might increase. But where sin increased, grace increased all the more, so that, just as sin reigned in death, so also grace might reign through righteousness to bring eternal life through Jesus Christ our Lord.

Galatians 2:16

So we, too, have put our faith in Christ Jesus that we may be justified by faith in Christ and not by the works of the law, because by the works of the law no one will be justified.

A summary of Paul's teaching on justification:

Being declared righteous by God is not earned through the works of the law, religious activity, or morality but is fully purchased for us* [redemption] *by Jesus through his blood and is freely given to us by God and is received by faith in Jesus.

JAMES' TEACHING ON JUSTIFICATION

James 2:14-26

What good is it, my brothers and sisters, if someone claims to have faith but has no deeds? Can such faith save them? Suppose a brother or a sister is without clothes and daily food. If one of you says to them, "Go in peace; keep warm and well fed," but does nothing about their physical needs, what good is it? In the same way, faith by itself, if it is not accompanied by action, is dead. But someone will say, "You have faith; I have deeds." Show me your faith without deeds, and I will show you my faith by my deeds. You believe that there is one God. Good! Even the demons believe that—and shudder. You foolish person, do you want evidence that faith without deeds is useless? Was not our father Abraham considered righteous for what he did when he offered his son Isaac on the altar? You see that his faith and his actions were working together, and his faith was made complete by what he did. And the scripture was fulfilled that says, "Abraham believed God, and it was credited to him as righteousness," and he was called God's friend. You see that a person is considered righteous by what they do and not by faith alone. In the same way, was not even Rahab the prostitute considered righteous for what she did when she gave lodging to the spies and sent them off in a different direction? As the body without the spirit is dead, so faith without deeds is dead.

A summary of James' teaching on justification:

Being declared righteous by God comes by a combination of one's faith and deeds working together.

PAUL MAKES IT CRYSTAL CLEAR

As we compare the Scriptures concerning Paul's and James' teachings on justification, Paul makes it ***crystal clear*** a person is justified by faith in Jesus alone, without faith and deeds working together. Notice, for example, in Ephesians 2:8-10 how Paul makes it very clear works play no role in our salvation, which is synonymous with justification.

*For it is by grace you have been saved, through faith - and this not from yourselves - it is the gift of God - **not by works**, so that no one can boast. For we are God's handiwork, created in Christ Jesus to do good works, which God prepared in advance for us to walk in.*

He also makes it very clear in Romans 4:5-8.

11

*However, to the one who does not work but trusts God who justifies the ungodly, their faith is credited as righteousness. David says the same thing when he speaks of the blessedness of the one to whom God credits righteousness **apart from works**:*

*"Blessed are those
whose transgressions are forgiven,
whose sins are covered.
Blessed is the one
whose sin the Lord will never count against them."*

JAMES MAKES IT CRYSTAL CLEAR

Whereas Paul makes it crystal clear works have no role at all in salvation or justification, James makes it crystal clear that justification comes from not just faith alone, but faith working together with deeds. Where Paul seeks to make it crystal clear to those reading his letters that works or deeds have **no role** in justification, only faith does, James seeks to make it crystal clear to those reading his letter that works and deeds each have a role in justification. We see this emphasis in James 2:24.

*You see that a person is considered righteous by **what they do and not by faith alone**.*

BIBLE TEACHERS AND PREACHERS WORK HARD

Because the teachings of both Paul and James on the subject of justification are obviously in conflict with one another, thus causing Scripture to seemingly be contradicting, Bible teachers and preachers work hard to harmonize the teachings of Paul and James, fearing disunity between their letters would cause the entire Bible to become untrustworthy. Therefore, driven by this fear, they teach the views of Paul and James in such a way so they appear to be in total agreement. In doing this, they come up with various interpretations and man-made illustrations to explain away the clear contradicting views of James and Paul on justification.

One popular illustration Bible teachers and preachers use to harmonize the teachings of James and Paul is to say that their teaching on justification is much like fire and smoke.

How do you know there is a fire in the fireplace? We know it because of the smoke coming out of the chimney. It is the fire that produces the smoke. The "fire" in the life of the believer is one's faith in his heart. The "smoke" is one's deeds in his life. Paul, in his letters, focuses on the fire in the fireplace...faith in one's heart. James, in his letter, focuses on the smoke in the chimney...one's deeds. So, therefore, Paul and James are in agreement.

Paul is saying to have faith in Jesus. James is saying that real faith produces deeds. So, like Paul says, we are justified by faith. Yet, what James says is true as well, real faith produces deeds. They are both in agreement. Paul simply focuses on the fire in the fireplace, and James focuses on the smoke coming from the chimney.

This is a nice illustration in attempting to reconcile Paul's and James' teachings. However, the illustration falls way short of what Paul and James are really teaching. James is not teaching that deeds are evidence of real faith. Rather, he plainly says deeds and faith work together to justify a person, a person's deeds complete his faith. Again, we must let Scripture speak for itself, rather than allowing preachers and Bible teachers to speak for Scripture by coming up with clever illustrations. So what does Scripture say? What does James say? What does Paul say?

James says:

You see that his faith and his actions were working together, and his faith was made complete by what he did (James 2:22).

You see that a person is considered righteous by what they do and not by faith alone (James 2:24).

Paul says:

*However, to the one who **does not work** but trusts God who justifies the ungodly, their faith is credited as righteousness (Romans 4:5).*

It is obvious Paul and James had vastly different understandings of justification. James' understanding of justification was that faith and deeds worked together to justify. Paul's understanding of justification was that faith alone justifies, apart from works.

WHEN WAS ABRAHAM JUSTIFIED?

In continuing to compare the letters of Paul with the letter of James concerning justification, we notice both refer to Abraham in supporting their views. James says Abraham was declared righteous by God as a result of his faith and actions working together, saying it was **when** Abraham obeyed God and offered his son Isaac on the altar that his faith was made complete and he was declared righteous.

*You foolish person, do you want evidence that faith without deeds is useless? **Was not our father Abraham considered righteous for what he did <u>when</u> he offered his son Isaac on the altar?** You see that his faith and his actions were working together, and his faith was made complete by what he did. And the scripture was fulfilled that says, "Abraham believed God, and it was credited to him as righteousness," and he was called God's friend. You see that a person is considered righteous by what they do and not by faith alone* (James 2:20-24).

Now, let's compare how Paul uses Abraham to support his teaching on justification.

What then shall we say that Abraham, our forefather according to the flesh, discovered in this matter? If, in fact, Abraham was justified by works, he had something to boast about—but not before God. What does Scripture say? "Abraham believed God, and it was credited to him as righteousness." Now to the one who works, wages are not credited as a gift but as an obligation. However, to the one who does not work but trusts God who justifies the ungodly, their faith is credited as righteousness (Romans 4:1-5).

So also Abraham "believed God, and it was credited to him as righteousness." Understand, then, that those who have faith are children of Abraham. Scripture foresaw that God would justify the Gentiles by faith, and announced the gospel in advance to Abraham: "All nations will be blessed through you." So those who rely on faith are blessed along with Abraham, the man of faith (Galatians 3:6-9).

Is this blessedness only for the circumcised, or also for the uncircumcised? We have been saying that Abraham's faith was credited to him as righteousness. Under what circumstances was it credited? Was it after he was circumcised, or before? It was not after, but before! And he received circumcision as a sign, a seal of the righteousness that he had by faith while he was still uncircumcised. So then, he is the father of all who believe but have not been circumcised, in order that righteousness might be credited to them. And he is then also the father of the circumcised who not only are circumcised but who also follow in the footsteps of the faith that our father Abraham had before he was circumcised. It was not through the law that Abraham and his offspring received the promise that he would be heir of the world, but through the righteousness that comes by faith. For if those who depend on the law are heirs, faith means nothing and the promise is worthless, because the law brings wrath. And where there is no law there is no transgression. Therefore, the promise comes by faith, so that it may be by grace and may be guaranteed to all Abraham's offspring—not only to those who are of the law but also to those who have the faith of Abraham. He is the father of us all. As it is written: "I have made you a father of many nations." He is our father in the sight of God, in whom he believed—the God who gives life to the dead and calls into being things that were not. Against all hope, Abraham in hope believed and so became the father of many nations, just as it had been said to him, "So shall your offspring be." Without weakening in his faith, he faced the fact that his body was as good as dead—since he was about a hundred years old—and that Sarah's womb was also dead. Yet he did not waver through unbelief regarding the promise of God, but was strengthened in his faith and gave glory to God, being fully persuaded that God had power to do what he had promised. This is why "it was credited to him as righteousness." The words "it was credited to him" were written not for him alone, but also for us, to whom God will credit righteousness—for us who believe in him who raised Jesus our Lord from the dead. He was delivered over to death for our sins and was raised to life for our justification (Romans 4:9-25).

Paul makes it very clear God credited righteousness to Abraham through faith. Paul proves through Scripture that God declared Abraham to be righteous **before** Isaac was even born. Genesis 15:4-6 says:

17

Then the word of the Lord came to him: "This man will not be your heir, but a son who is your own flesh and blood will be your heir." He took him outside and said, "Look up at the sky and count the stars—if indeed you can count them." Then he said to him, "So shall your offspring be." Abram believed the Lord, and he credited it to him as righteousness.

James, using the exact verse Paul used, says God credited righteousness to Abraham **when** he offered Isaac. However, James takes this verse out of context to support his point that faith and deeds work together to bring justification. He associates Genesis 15:6 with God crediting righteousness to Abraham **when he offered Isaac**. However, in Genesis 15:6, Isaac was not even born yet!

Based upon Scripture itself, God declared Abraham to be righteous **when Abraham believed a son would be born to him and before Isaac was born**. This is the point Paul makes to support his view that faith alone apart from works is how God declares a person to be righteous. By using Genesis 15:6 in this way, Paul keeps this verse in proper historical context, whereas James moves the verse anywhere from 13 to 35 years later to the time when Abraham offered Isaac, since it was likely that Isaac was between the ages of 12 and 35 when the offering took place.

So following this timeline, Paul has God crediting righteousness to Abraham around age 85, whereas James has God crediting righteous to Abraham somewhere between ages 112 and 145. That's quite a difference in the age and timing Paul and James say righteousness was credited to Abraham, and quite a difference in theology, too! I don't think the *fire in the fireplace* and *smoke in the chimney* illustration supports the harmony of the vast differences between Paul and James no matter how hard Bible teachers work at making it do so.

THE ISSUE OF BELIEVES

Another issue Paul and James seem to disagree on is that of **believes**. In Paul's first recorded missionary journey and sermon, he is quoted by Luke as saying (Acts 13:38-39):

*Therefore let it be known to you, brothers, that through Jesus the forgiveness of sins is proclaimed to you. Through Him everyone who **believes** is justified from everything you could not be justified from by the law of Moses.*

Paul's use of the word *believes* was dominate in his presentations of the good news of God's grace. In his letters, he uses the words believe, believes, believers, believed over 40 times when talking about a person responding to his message of salvation or justification through Jesus alone.

Because so many Jews were scattered throughout the cites Paul traveled to testify about the good news of God's grace, news that Paul was communicating an "easy-believism" gospel would have traveled back to Jerusalem quickly by AD 44. This prompted James to correct Paul's "easy-believism" teaching by writing in his letter:

But someone will say, "You have faith and I have deeds."
Show me your faith without deeds, and I will show you my
faith by my deeds. You believe that God is one. Good for
you! Even the demons believe that—and shudder. (James
2:18-19)

It seems obvious Paul's and James' teachings on the topic
of believe is much different. James seems to be doing
what many do today, attacking the gospel of grace as
easy-believism. He seems to be even mocking Paul's
teaching of *believe*.

Before the crucifixion, resurrection, and
ascension of Jesus, people asked Jesus what good works
they needed to do to gain eternal life. Jesus said the work
of God was to believe (John 6:27-29). The word believe is
used over 80 times in the book of John, none are
combined with works. The message of believe apart from
works was the message of Jesus, John, and Paul. James
seems to be taking a different position on *believe* by
adding works.

A SCRIPTURAL EXPLANATION
OF THE DIFFERING VIEWS OF PAUL AND JAMES

Maybe it is the intention of man to seek to find
agreement between Paul and James on their teachings
on justification, but maybe it is not God's intention. Could
it be man's intention is not God's intention? Could it be
there is a Scriptural explanation for why Paul and James
have such vast differences? Could understanding this
conflict between Paul and James give us greater
understanding of the Bible?

We will let Scripture speak to this.

SOME THINGS TO KNOW ABOUT JAMES

Many people are surprised to learn the very first book or letter written in the New Testament is James, thus making it the oldest book or letter in the New Testament. The letter of James was written around A.D. 44.

James was the brother of Jesus and remained an unbeliever in Jesus (John 7:3-5) until after the resurrection (Acts 1:14; 1 Corinthians 15:7; Galatians 1:19), eventually becoming the leader of the Jewish church in Jerusalem (Acts 15:13; 21:17-18; Galatians 2:9). The Jewish church consisted of those who had come to believe in Jesus as the Christ, the One promised by God in the Jewish Scriptures who would be Savior-King. This large group of believers had repented (Acts 2:16-38) of denying Jesus as the Christ and having him turned over to Rome for crucifixion (John 19). In following Jewish custom, they acknowledged through baptism their repentance and belief in Jesus as the Christ (Acts 2:38).

SOME THINGS TO KNOW ABOUT PAUL

As a leading Pharisee in Jerusalem, Paul, also known as Saul (Acts 9:1), was convinced Jesus was not the Christ, and he should do everything he could to halt this Messianic Jesus movement (Acts 26:9-11). Angry at the large number of Jewish people turning to Jesus as the Christ, Paul began violently persecuting and imprisoning these believers, even putting some of them to death (Acts 8:1-3; 9:1; 22:4). As a result of the persecution by Paul and other religious leaders, the believers scattered in fear (Acts 8:1).

As the believers scattered, the message of Jesus begin to spread. Determined to stop the spread of this Jesus movement, and to eradicate it completely from the face of the earth, Paul set out for Damascus. While on his way, the ascended Jesus appeared to him (Acts 9). Paul describes this encounter with Jesus as the time when God's grace, faith, and love was poured upon him abundantly (1 Timothy 1:13-14).

Following this encounter, the ascended Jesus announced to Paul the gospel of grace and the message of faith, which was that by faith in Jesus forgiveness and righteousness are received (Acts 26:18). This was the core of Paul's teachings.

Paul made it very clear the gospel of grace he preached was given to him by direct revelation from the ascended Jesus himself.

*However, I consider my life worth nothing to me; my only aim is to finish the race and complete **the task the Lord Jesus has given me**—the task of testifying to the **gospel of God's grace*** (Acts 20:24).

*I want you to know, brothers and sisters, that the gospel I preached is not of human origin. I did not receive it from any man, nor was I taught it; rather, **I received it by revelation from Jesus Christ*** (Galatians 1:11).

PAUL WAS GIVEN THE REVELATION OF GRACE

The message the ascended Jesus gave Paul was the good news of grace. The good news of grace is that God desires to be in a relationship with us. He is no longer counting our sins against us, because they were all counted against Jesus. Therefore, there is no sin-barrier preventing a person from knowing God personally. Jesus became sin for us so by faith in him we would become righteous and reconciled to God. This the message of which Paul was an ambassador, speaking on behalf of Jesus himself (2 Corinthians 5:18-6:2).

Teh mission given to Paul by Jesus was to take the message of grace to the Gentiles (Acts 22:21; 26:15-18; Ephesians 3:1-13). As Paul went into the Gentile cities all over the Roman Empire, he would proclaim the good news of God's grace. Those who responded by faith to the message of all God had freely done for them in Jesus for forgiveness and righteousness became a local church, or a group of believers in Jesus who had received his grace by faith and became a community of grace within their city.

Scattered among the Gentile cities where Paul proclaimed the message of grace, given to him by direct revelation from the ascended Jesus, were Jewish people. Not only had the Jews been scattered among the Gentile cities as a result of the persecution of Saul and other Jewish leaders in the early chapters of Acts, but the Jewish people had been scattered among the nations for about 650 years as a result of Babylon invading Jerusalem in 605 BC. The other scattering occurred in Acts 12 when King Herod began persecuting believers.

As Paul and his companions began sharing the good news of God's grace among the Gentiles, the scattered Jews began to hear the good news of grace as well. The good news being through faith or belief in Jesus one is justified, or declared righteous by God (Acts 13).

As the good news of God's grace spread, the Jewish religious leaders tracked Paul down and persecuted him, attacking both Paul and the message of grace. This is evident in the book of Acts during Paul's missionary journeys.

PAUL'S LETTER TO THE GALATIANS

This prompted Paul to write letters back to churches and to local pastors of those churches, establishing them more deeply in the good news of grace and encouraging them to stand strong in grace. One of these letters he wrote was to the Galatian churches.

In Galatians 2:12, we discover specific men came from James, the same James who wrote the letter of James, to Antioch from Jerusalem to challenge Paul's message of grace, telling the believers justification came by faith plus works. These specific men sent from James were so persuasive in their attacks on grace even Peter and Barnabas were led astray from the truth that one is justified freely by grace through faith in Jesus alone, apart from works (Galatians 2:11-13).

Some Bible teachers, in their attempts to make a case that James and Paul saw eye to eye on justification, say James did not send these men personally to Antioch, but these men came entirely on their own, with no support from James at all. They may very well be right in their view. But the questions I have is why did Paul mention James at all if these men came down totally on their own? Why would Paul have not clarified in the text, or more clearly stated, these men had no support from James and had not been sent by him? Why would Paul even connect James to these specific men if James had no connection with them coming to Antioch and causing confusion among the people by disputing the teaching of Paul on justification? It seems to me, from the text, Paul is purposefully and clearly connecting these men with James, leading us to believe James had total knowledge and was in full support of what these men were teaching. Not only does the text support James was fully supportive of these men, but he personally selected and sent these men to Antioch. Why else would Paul mention these certain men came from James?

With this in mind, let's take a look in Galatians 2:11-21 at Paul's response to Peter when he deserted the truth of justification by grace through faith in Jesus for justification and embraced a combination of works and faith promoted by the specific men sent from James.

*When Peter came to Antioch, I opposed him to his face, because he stood condemned. **For before certain men came from James**, he used to eat with the Gentiles. But when they arrived, he began to draw back and separate himself from the Gentiles because he was afraid of those who belonged to the circumcision group. The other Jews joined him in his hypocrisy, so that by their hypocrisy even Barnabas was led astray. When I saw that they were not acting in line with the truth of the gospel, I said to Cephas [Peter] in front of them all, "You are a Jew, yet you live like a Gentile and not like a Jew. How is it, then, that you force Gentiles to follow Jewish customs? "We who are*

Jews by birth and not sinful Gentiles know that a person is not justified by the works of the law, but by faith in Jesus Christ. So we, too, have put our faith in Christ Jesus that we may be justified by faith in Christ and not by the works of the law, because by the works of the law no one will be justified. But if, in seeking to be justified in Christ, we Jews find ourselves also among the sinners, doesn't that mean that Christ promotes sin? Absolutely not! If I rebuild what I destroyed, then I really would be a lawbreaker. For through the law I died to the law so that I might live for God. I have been crucified with Christ and I no longer live, but Christ lives in me. The life I now live in the body, I live by faith in the Son of God, who loved me and gave himself for me. I do not set aside the grace of God, for if righteousness could be gained through the law, Christ died for nothing!"

As we see in these verses, Paul was passionate about justification by grace through faith in Jesus alone. When we read Paul's letters, it is clear there is no mixture of deeds and faith working together to complete one's faith. Directly from the ascended Jesus to Paul, justification is by grace through faith in Jesus alone (Galatians 1:11-12).

In comparing Paul's and James' views of justification, it is obvious and clear their views are different. Again, James says a person is justified by faith and deeds working together (James 2:24) compared to Paul who says a person is justified by faith apart from works (Romans 4:5).

SHOULD WE GET RID OF THE BIBLE?

So the questions are, "Do the different views on justification between Paul and James cause such a contradiction in the Bible that they render the Bible untrustworthy, as many Bible teachers and preachers would lead us to believe? Do the opposing views of Paul and James necessitate getting rid of the Bible all together?

Let's answer these questions.

The Bible is the unfolding of God's plan of grace that existed before time began (2 Timothy 1:9). As the message of God's grace unfolds over the course of time, requirements of God in one age are no longer required in another age, such as with food. What Adam and Eve could eat in one age was different from what the people of Israel could eat in another. Eventually, what the people of Israel could eat in one age was no longer applicable in another age. For example, in Acts 10 God gave Peter a vision, allowing him to eat anything. This was in direct contradiction with the requirements of food God had previously given in other ages. This does not mean the Bible is in contradiction with itself, but simply God made changes over time in the unfolding of his plan of grace to the human race.

Another change was that before the cross of Jesus, Jews were not allowed into the homes of Gentiles. After the cross of Jesus and his resurrection, Jews were allowed into the homes of Gentiles. This change, too, is seen in Acts 10 when, through Peter's God-given vision, the Spirit revealed to him he was to go into the home of Cornelius, a Gentile.

These changes by God were not always immediately accepted. Some rejected the changes. Some accepted the changes. For others, it took much time to make the transition between God's old way of law and his new way of grace. This was especially true with the old covenant of law and the new covenant of grace. Some rejected the new covenant of grace. Some accepted the new covenant of grace. For some, there was a transition from living under law to living under grace. The vision God gave Peter in Acts 10, confirming the new covenant of grace by showing him he could eat all foods and then having him go to a Gentile's home, reveals the difficult transition Peter, as well as many others, had moving from living under the old covenant of law to living under the new covenant of grace. As a matter of fact, Peter stepped in and out of, or straddled, the covenants, depending upon what religious leaders he was around. His vision to eat any food and to enter a Gentile's house was around AD 40, which is seven years after Jesus established the new covenant in his blood. Peter's lapse back into the law in Antioch could have been as late as AD 53.

It was this difficult transition from law to grace that created great discussions and debates following the ascension of Jesus. The debates centered around the issue of justification. The religious leaders debated whether a person is justified by grace through faith alone or if a person is justified by faith and deeds working together, deeds based upon the Law of Moses and that followed circumcision.

The Jerusalem Council

The issue of justification was such a hot topic that an official meeting was held in Jerusalem among the leaders to discuss and debate the topic (Acts 15). James and Paul were both in attendance. This meeting took place between AD 48-50 and has been called The Jerusalem Council. After much debate and discussion, the matter was settled. Salvation or justification is by grace through faith alone (Acts 15:11).

The date of The Jerusalem Council is important. The council was held between A.D. 48-50, which is after the letter James wrote to the scattered Jewish people and before Paul's letter to the Galatians. Paul refers to this council in Galatians 2:1-10.

During the six-year period between the letters of James and Paul, discussion and debate on the issue of justification was fierce. It was so fierce that Paul was persecuted greatly by those on the other side of the debate. They were constantly seeking to discredit his teaching of grace. For example, in seeking to discredit Paul's grace teachings, James sent men from Jerusalem to Antioch to teach that justification comes by faith plus the works of the law (Galatians 2:12). It wasn't until after The Jerusalem Council that they finally came into agreement that salvation, or justification, is by grace through faith. However, Scripture and early church history indicates James remained zealous for the Mosaic Law, and as the leader of the Jerusalem Messianic church, he continued to lead the church to practice many elements of the law, including obedience to the Great Commandment for justification: "Love your neighbor as you love yourself."

This is the same commandment the Pharisees and teachers of the law prided themselves on as they tried to justify themselves and is what prompted Jesus to tell *The Story of the Good Samaritan*.

In this story, the teacher of the Law thought obedience to the commandment, "Love your neighbor as you love yourself" would justify him, make him righteous before God, so he could enter into eternal life in God's future kingdom. So Jesus, using this commandment, revealed the hateful heart of the teacher of the law by proving he hated the Samaritan, thus disqualifying himself entrance into the kingdom, since he failed to obey the law.

Love Your Neighbor

James, in his letter, does not focus on works of the law for justification; rather, he focuses on one of the two Great Commandments of the Mosaic Law for justification: "Love your neighbor as you love yourself."

If you really keep the royal law found in Scripture, "Love your neighbor as yourself," you are doing right. But if you show favoritism, you sin and are convicted by the law as lawbreakers. For whoever keeps the whole law and yet stumbles at just one point is guilty of breaking all of it. For he who said, "You shall not commit adultery," also said, "You shall not murder." If you do not commit adultery but do commit murder, you have become a lawbreaker. Speak and act as those who are going to be judged by the law that gives freedom, because judgment without mercy will be shown to anyone who has not been merciful. Mercy triumphs over judgment. (James 2:8-13)

The works James proposes are the works of love based upon the Great Commandment, "Love your neighbor as you love yourself." In James' understanding of justification, it was a combination of faith and love for one's neighbor that would work together to justify a sinner. This sounds much like the Judaizes in Antioch and Galatia teaching that faith plus circumcision is what justifies someone.

In his letter, James makes no mention of the new commandment of Jesus: "Love one another as I have loved you." This new commandment of love replaced the two old commandments of love that were based upon the Law of Moses. The new commandment of love Jesus established was based upon his love for humanity demonstrated at the cross. This new commandment was to be practiced by the new covenant community as they experienced the love of Jesus. James was still pre-occupied with the old commandment of the Mosaic Law, which no one could fulfill, rather than on the new commandment of Jesus, which only the Spirit indwelling a believer's heart could fulfill.

In Galatians, Paul also teaches on the Great Commandment "Love your neighbor as you love yourself." Paul teaches that what matters most is faith expressing itself in love (Galatians 5:6). However, Paul makes it clear that justification is not a result of faith and love working together. He says the love flowing from a person is the result of the Spirit-filled life, where a person has been removed from the law, and the Spirit of Jesus now indwells this person, allowing him to call God "*Abba Father*" (Galatians 4:4-6). The result of the Spirit-filled life is that a person is no longer led by the law externally but is lead internally by the Spirit to experience the Father's love and to love others (Galatians 5:18).

Paul says by walking in the Spirit one will fulfill the law "to love your neighbor as yourself" (Galatians 5:13-14). Furthermore, Paul says the Spirit, as we walk in a love relationship with the Father and not according to the law, will produce in us love, resulting in joy, peace, patience, kindness, goodness, gentleness, faithfulness, and self-control (Galatians 5:22-23). He states there is no law needed when one is walking in the love produced by the Spirit. Whereas Paul teaches love is the fruit of the Spirit, James makes no mention of the Spirit-filled life.

So what we find is Paul and James both teach on love and justification, yet from two different viewpoints. Paul makes it clear **love is the eventual result of justification** that comes by grace through faith, where the Spirit comes to live in a person's heart and produces love as a person grows in a love relationship with the Father. However, James says **justification is the result of love** and faith working together. He makes no mention of the Spirit or knowing God as Father, which empowers a person to love others.

SO WHY WOULD GOD ALLOW
THE BOOK OF JAMES INTO THE BIBLE?

So why would God allow the book of James into the Bible if it is in contradiction to the teaching of Paul on justification, a teaching given directly to him by the ascended Jesus (Galatians 1:11-12)?

The letter of James, the book of Acts, and Paul's letters give us an insightful and historical look into the difficult transition from law to grace James and others experienced during the early church years. James' struggle with faith and works relating to justification was real, just as it is today for many people. His struggle with the issue of *believes* was real, just as it is for many today.

Discussions and debates over law and grace, faith and works, and easy-believism continue today. The struggle continues. It was no different then than it is now. Why would we assume it would be? God, in the Bible, shows us this historic struggle...this transition. This is why God allowed the letter of James into the Bible. We do not have to be afraid nor surprised of the fact that Paul and James had different views on justification. We do not have to attempt to explain their views in such a way as to make their views seem complementary, harmonizing together perfectly. God allows us to see directly into their differences through their letters, and by doing so captures historically in the Bible the difficulty the early church had transitioning from the Law of Moses to the Grace of Jesus.

By properly studying the Bible and the dates the letters of James and Paul were written, it becomes quite clear there was an early struggle over the issue of justification, resulting in very heated discussions and debates. However, as we continue to study, we see the issue was eventually settled in Acts 15 (AD 48-50), which was after the letter of James was written (AD 44) but before the letter of Galatians was written. And what did they settle on in Acts 15...justification by grace alone through faith alone!

PAUL'S LETTERS CONTAIN THE
LARGER REVELATIONS OF GRACE

C.I. Scofield, a highly respected Bible teacher during the late 1800s and early 1900s, stated in his notes in the *C.I. Scofield Study Bible 1917 Edition* that the letter of James *"shows no trace of the larger revelations concerning the church and the distinctive doctrines of grace made through the Apostle Paul"* and that James' letter *"is elementary in the extreme."*

C.I Scofield understood the unfolding of grace during the early days of Paul and James was a transition period from law to grace, and the letter James wrote was during a time when the larger truths of grace revealed by the ascended Jesus to Paul had not yet been fully grasped by many people. Jesus, through Paul, communicated the larger revelations of grace.

Paul called the larger revelations of grace given to him by the ascended Jesus a mystery. He was given by Jesus the responsibility and gift of teaching the revelation of God's grace.

Surely you have heard about the administration of God's grace that was given to me for you, that is, the mystery made known to me by revelation, as I have already written briefly. In reading this, then, you will be able to understand my insight into the mystery of Christ, which was not made known to people in other generations as it has now been revealed by the Spirit to God's holy apostles and prophets. This mystery is that through the gospel the Gentiles are heirs together with Israel, members together of one body, and sharers together in the promise in Christ Jesus. I became a servant of this gospel by the gift of God's grace given me through the working of his power. Although I am less than the least of all the Lord's people, this grace was given me: to preach to the Gentiles the boundless riches of Christ, and to make plain to everyone the administration of this mystery, which for ages past was kept hidden in God, who created all things (Ephesians 3:2-9).

Notice in the verses above that Paul says the Spirit has *now revealed to the holy apostles and prophets* the mystery of Christ, the boundless riches of God's grace that brought Jew and Gentile together into one body, without the Law of Moses (Ephesians 2:11-22; 3:3-9).

The *now* he is referring to would be at the time of Paul writing his letter to the Ephesians, around 60-62 A.D. Paul had earlier insight into God's grace than the other apostles and prophets. They did not have this understanding until much later. Paul's revelation of grace started in A.D. 33 when Jesus appeared to him and began giving him revelations of the larger truths of grace, which we see in Romans, 2 Corinthians 3-6:2, Galatians, Ephesians, Philippians, and Colossians. All of these letters were written after the letter of James. The revelation to the apostles came years later.

With this understanding of Scripture, James had yet to come to the full revelation of grace at the time his letter was written. The Spirit had not yet given the full revelation to James. That is why his letter does not contain the fuller revelations of grace and is elementary in nature, as C.I Scofield identifies. It is debatable if James truly came to embrace the full revelation of grace, where Jew and Gentile made up the body of Christ, the church, which the law had no place at all. According to the revelation of grace given to Paul by Jesus, the law was abolished (Ephesians 2:15) and Jews and Gentiles were now united into one body...one family of grace!

WE MUST ALLOW FOR THE
UNFOLDING AND UNDERSTANDING OF GRACE

In correctly interpreting James, we must allow time for the unfolding and understanding of the full revelation of grace, which Jesus initially revealed to Paul, and Paul taught others. We must allow time for believers, including James, to transition from law to grace.

Grace is the total accomplishments of Jesus on the cross for the forgiveness of all our sins and cleansing from all unrighteousness. We must allow time for people to understand the Spirit-filled life under the new covenant, which is the Spirit coming into the hearts of those who place their faith in Jesus, where they call God "Abba Father."

It was to Paul the complete revelation of grace initially and progressively came, which he eventually revealed to others. The revelation of grace given to Paul was difficult for the early church to understand, including James. Even Peter admits having difficulty understanding Paul's letters.

Bear in mind that our Lord's patience means salvation, just as our dear brother Paul also wrote you with the wisdom that God gave him. He writes the same way in all his letters, speaking in them of these matters. His letters contain some things that are hard to understand, which ignorant and unstable people distort, as they do the other Scriptures, to their own destruction (2 Peter 3:15-16).

Peter wrote 2 Peter around A.D. 65. This shows the difficulty people had in understanding grace, even after 32 years following the resurrection and ascension of Jesus and his revelation of grace to Paul. According to Peter, some ignorant and unstable people took Jesus' message of grace communicated through Paul as a license to sin. Using grace as a license to sin was what Peter taught on in 2 Peter 2 as well as what Jude addressed in his letter (Jude 4).

The difficulty people had understanding grace during the time of James, Peter, and Paul is the same today. People have a difficult time understanding grace. Many have a difficult time understanding it is by grace through faith alone, without works, that God declares a person righteous.

CORRECTLY INTERPRETING THE LETTER OF JAMES

Now that we have allowed Scripture to give us insight into the differing viewpoints of Paul and James on justification, we have a greater understanding of the James' letter within its historical context. This doesn't mean James' letter does not have valuable truths. There are truths within his letter we can apply to our lives.

However, we must interpret the letter of James in accordance to God's gradual unfolding of grace through Paul to the world, allowing for the difficulty and struggle many had in understanding and fully embracing the revelation of God's grace.

We must approach the letter of James just as we do the Jewish Scriptures. There is much in the Jewish Scriptures that are encouraging to us as Paul says in Romans 15:4. However, they must be interpreted in light of the new covenant of grace and the mystery about the church given to Paul by the ascended Jesus.

According to the Bible, the new covenant of grace replaced the old covenant of law. As a result, not everything written in the Jewish Scriptures is applicable to us. But some of it is beneficial to us, as long as we first interpret it correctly.

We must interpret Scripture by differentiating between Jesus' ministry to Israel under the old covenant of law and his establishment of the new covenant of grace through his blood, which the writer of Hebrews expounds upon. Additionally, we must distinguish between the prophecies for the nation of Israel and the mystery of the church that Jesus, following his ascension, revealed to Paul.

This is the same approach we must use when interpreting the letter of James. When reading the letter of James, we must allow the fuller revelation of justification by grace through faith alone, given by the ascended Jesus to Paul, replace the elementary teachings of justification by faith and works proposed by James. We must interpret James through the truths of Romans, 1 and 2 Corinthians, Galatians, Ephesians, Philippians,

Colossians, Hebrews, 1 and 2 Thessalonians, 1 and 2 Timothy, and Titus. These letters contain the fuller revelations of the new covenant of grace and the mystery of the church given by the ascended Jesus to Paul.

We must follow Jesus' words to the Pharisees and teachers of the law in their approach to studying Scripture. According to Jesus, in their approach to studying Scripture, they missed what it was all about, the coming of Jesus as the Christ to establish the new covenant (John 5:39). We must take into account when interpreting and applying Scripture the gradual unfolding and understanding of the new covenant of grace and the mystery of the church. We can't miss this. If we miss this, we will totally misunderstand and misapply the Bible. We must follow Paul's advice to Timothy to accurately teach and apply God's word by correctly studying it.

By following the words of Jesus to the Pharisees and teachers of the law in studying the Bible and by following the advice of Paul to Timothy in studying the Bible, we will have a more accurate understanding of the letter of James in comparison with the letters of Paul when it comes to understanding justification. We will no longer need to force into harmony these two opposing viewpoints on justification or make them complementary of one another. We can now allow them to be what they are: historical insight into the difficult struggle many had transitioning from the old covenant of law to the new covenant of grace and from the nation of Israel under the law to the church (Jew and Gentile in one body, without the law) under grace, which Paul called a mystery.

ABOUT THE AUTHOR

In 1991, the story of God's grace intersected with the story of Brad's life when he read a book by Bob George called *Classic Christianity*. Since this time, his passion has been to share the life-changing truths of God's grace with as many people as possible in as many ways as possible. Some of the ways Brad shares the good news of God's grace is through writing, social media, and speaking.

In addition to this booklet, Brad has written **The Story of Grace**, **Addicted To Grace**, and **Strategic Church**. He has also written commentaries on Romans, Galatians, and Philippians All of his writings are available on his website or Amazon. Brad's website is: www.simplygrace.info.

In addition to his books, Brad has many other resources on his website to help you grow in grace. There you will find his podcast, video teachings, and many blogs he has written, as well as links to other grace teachers. You may also visit his YouTube channel and Facebook page.

For 13 years, Brad served as founder and Senior Pastor of Grace Church Gulf Coast. Prior to this, he attended Dallas Theological Seminary, where he received a Master of Arts Degree in Christian Education. In addition, he served on staff with Campus Crusade for Christ for two years. He holds a Bachelor of Science Degree in Coaching and Sports Administration from the University of Southern Mississippi. He is married to Becky. Together they have three sons, Kyle, Philip, and Mark.

If you would like to contact Brad about speaking at your church, conference, retreat, or event, email him at bradr1966@gmail.com.

Printed in Great Britain
by Amazon

49647303R00031